MW01140113

ASTEROIDS, COMETS AND METEORS

CHILDREN'S SCIENCE & NATURE

BABY PROFESSOR

EDUCATION KIDS

Speedy Publishing LLC

40 E. Main St. #1156

Newark, DE 19711

www.speedypublishing.com

Copyright 2016

I love the night sky. I gaze into its endless depths. I've always been eager to look for "shooting stars" or "falling stars". Well, that's what my grandma calls them.

Normally, the lights in the night are just steadily twinkling up in the blanket of the heavens.

But when I see one amazing streak of light flash by, I make a wish.

But do you ever wonder
what those streaks of
light really are?
What are they made of?
Why do they seem to
shine?

Those flashes of light are made by chunks of rock and ice that are racing through space. That's pretty amazing, even if they are not actual stars.

The chunks come in different names. I remember my science teacher used to enumerate them: asteroids, comets, and meteors.

And I asked myself, "Huhhh...uhm...aren't they all one and the same?" I was confused. Blank. Void like space.

So now, I understand some of the differences and why it's wiser to define and differentiate the many sources of the flashes in the sky.

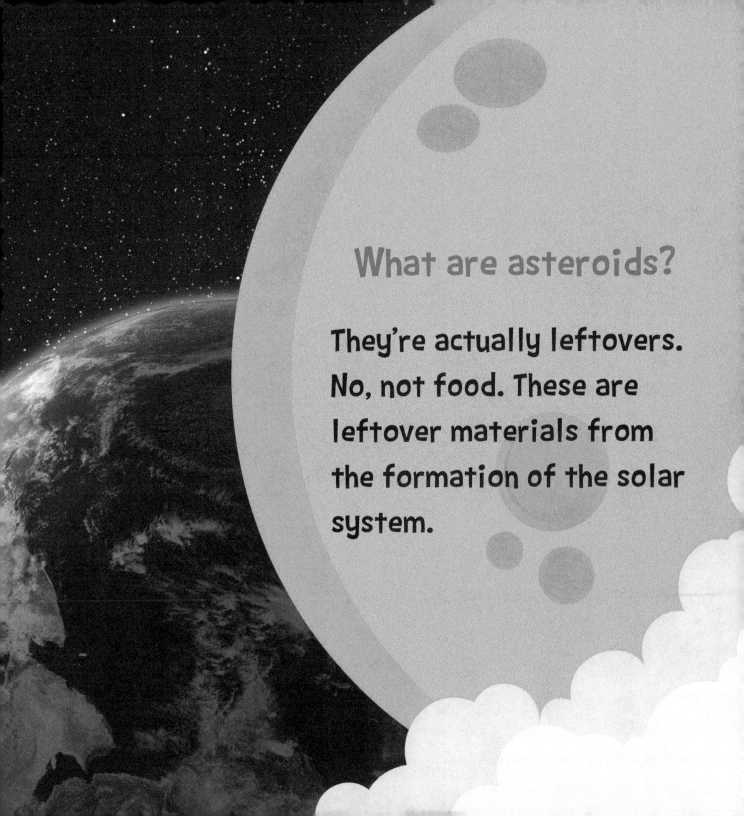

What are asteroids?

They're actually leftovers.
No, not food. These are
leftover materials from
the formation of the solar
system.

Asteroids are like large rocks in outer space. Some are quite large in size, like a truck or a house, others are small like grains of sand.

They actually reflect sunlight. And when they pass close to the Earth and touch the outer edge of our atmosphere, friction heats them very quickly and they glow brightly as they burn up. Onto the next...we have comets.

What are comets, really?

Comets are the brightest objects that pass close to the Earth. These rare objects of the night sky have tails! Yes, you read it right. Comet tails! But how? I wonder...

Comets are actually made of dust and ice, like a snowball you make in winter but much bigger and much older. The point of the comet's tail depends on where the sun's heat and radiation is.

As a comet gets closer to the sun, the solar wind will blow away some of the melted gas and dust off the comet.

And so there appears to be a "tail" on the side of the comet facing away from the sun.

Last, we have meteors.
These are "baby" versions
of asteroids. They're small
rocks or debris particles.
These burn up as they
pass through the earth's
atmosphere.

They glow brightly in the sky as they fall here from outer space. Such an awesome sight! Think of all three.

Now you know that, while
you might sometime
see a piece of a meteor
(a meteorite), you will
probably never see a piece
of a comet. However varied
they may seem, up above
the skies, they're simply
beautiful!

And since legend has it that wishing upon a shooting star makes the wish come true, regardless of which one you see tonight...just make a wish!

Visit

BABY PROFESSOR
EDUCATION KIDS

www.BabyProfessorBooks.com

to download Free Baby Professor eBooks
and view our catalog of new and exciting
Children's Books

CPSIA information can be obtained
at www.ICGtesting.com
Printed in the USA
LVHW051330040622
720440LV00006B/629